NATIONAL GEOGRAPHIC KiDS

T0318116

OUR WORLD Quiz Book

Published by Collins
An imprint of HarperCollins Publishers
Westerhill Road
Bishopbriggs
Glasgow G64 2QT
www.harpercollins.co.uk

HarperCollins Publishers
Macken House, 39/40 Mayor Street Upper,
Dublin 1, D01 C9W8, Ireland

In association with National Geographic
Partners, LLC

NATIONAL GEOGRAPHIC and the Yellow Border
Design are trademarks of the National
Geographic Society and used under license.

First published 2021

If you would like to comment on any aspect of
this book, please contact us at the above address
or online.
natgeokidsbooks.co.uk
collins.reference@harpercollins.co.uk

Acknowledgements
Text by Richard Happer

Images
P76: Ross Edgley image © Luke Walker/Stringer
/Getty Images

All other images © Shutterstock.com

MIX
Paper | Supporting
responsible forestry
FSC
www.fsc.org
FSC™ C007454

NATIONAL GEOGRAPHIC KiDS

OUR WORLD Quiz Book

300
brain busting
trivia questions

Contents

Volcanoes 6

Wild weather 10

Continents 14

Oceans 18

Earthquakes 22

Countries 26

Mountain ranges 30

Rivers 34

Capital cities 38

Ships and boats 42

Aircraft and airports 46

National flags 50

Abandoned places 54

World wonders 58

Waterfalls 62

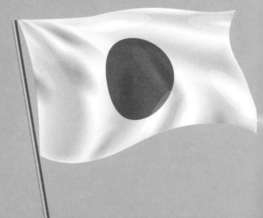

Traditions and celebrations 66

Food 70

Amazing journeys 74

Brilliant buildings 78

Deserts 82

Islands 86

10 of the biggest 90

Frozen poles 94

Connect four 98

Computers and technology 102

Transport 106

Sport 110

Elements 114

Bridges and tunnels 118

Mega machines 122

Tie breaker 126

VOLCANOES

1 Volcanoes only appear on land.
True or false?

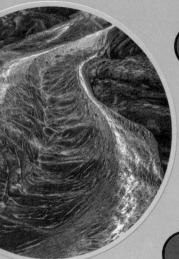

2 Which ancient Roman city was totally covered by volcanic ash in 79 AD and is now one of the most popular tourist attractions in Italy?
a. Milan   b. Venice   c. Pompeii

3 What is the flow of molten rock from a volcano called?
a. Lava   b. Ash   c. Java

4 When the Eyjafjallajökull volcano in Iceland erupted in 2010, it stopped planes from flying over most of Europe.
True or false?

5 What is a dormant volcano?
a. A volcano that has never erupted
b. A volcano that erupted 2 years ago
c. A volcano that has erupted in the last 10,000 years but is unlikely to erupt soon

6 Magma and lava are the same substance.
True or false?

7 Mauna Loa is a volcano in which US state?
a. Hawaii
b. New York
c. Florida

8 'Volcano' comes from the Roman name 'Vulcan'. Was Vulcan...
a. The god of fire?
b. The god of chocolate?
c. The god of geography?

9 Edinburgh Castle is built on an extinct volcano.
True or false?

10 What is the name for the crater left after a volcano erupts?
a. Scoop
b. Caldera
c. Black hole

VOLCANOES

1 **False.** Volcanoes also appear on the sea floor.

2 **c.** The eruption of Mount Vesuvius was a tragedy for Pompeii, but the ash preserved the city, giving us a fascinating snapshot of what life was like 2000 years ago.

3 **a.** The molten rock from a volcano eruption is known as lava.

4 **True.** The eruption of Eyjafjallajökull threw a huge ash cloud into the air, which was then spread by the wind. The tiny granules in volcanic ash are extremely bad news for jet engines, so hundreds of planes were grounded.

5 **c.** Dormant volcanoes are unlikely to erupt any time soon, but it can't be ruled out completely.

6 **False.** Magma is the substance below the surface of a volcano, but it's lava when it is above the surface.

7 **a.** Mauna Loa is Earth's largest active volcano! It covers around half of the island of Hawaii.

8 **a.** Vulcan was the Roman god of fire.

9 **True.** The volcano erupted about 340 million years ago.

10 **b.** After the magma inside the volcano is ejected, the chamber that held it often collapses and creates a cauldron-like crater called a caldera.

WILD WEATHER

1

What is one name for a storm that starts over tropical waters?

a. Tropstorm

b. Tsunami

c. Typhoon

2

What is it called when a huge amount of rain falls in a short time?

a. Zip flood

b. Rip tide

c. Flash flood

3

What is a fast-spinning column of air called?

a. Tornado

b. Whirlpool

c. Speedwind

4

The highest temperature ever recorded was 56.7 °C at Furnace Creek. Where is Furnace Creek?

a. Fury Island, Australia

b. Death Valley, USA

c. Cape Wrath, Scotland

5

Hail falls from very tall thunderclouds. Hailstones are usually at least 5 mm in diameter, but how big were the largest hailstones ever recorded?

a. As big as a marble

b. As big as a golf ball

c. As big as a volleyball

6

Japan is the snowiest country in the world.

True or false?

7

What makes Lake Maracaibo in Venezuela so unusual?

a. It has no water in it.

b. It gets struck by lightning more than any other place.

c. Its water is bright pink.

8

A lightning bolt is actually only about as wide as your thumb, but how hot is it?

a. Five times hotter than an oven on full power.

b. Five times hotter than a blow torch.

c. Five times hotter than the Sun.

9

The lowest natural temperature ever recorded on Earth is −89.2°C in 1983. Where was this?

a. Antarctica

b. The Sahara Desert

c. Aberdeen

10

Which country has the most tornadoes?

a. Spain

b. United Kingdom

c. United States

WILD WEATHER

1

c. Typhoons are rotating systems of clouds and thunderstorms that start over tropical waters.

2

c. Flash floods can be more dangerous than hurricanes or tornadoes because people underestimate their power—just 60 cm of water is enough to carry away a large car.

3

a. Tornadoes are the fastest winds on Earth!

4

b. Although it is far inland, Death Valley is 86 m below sea level.

5

c. The largest hailstones ever recorded were 20 cm in diameter and fell in South Dakota, USA, in 2010.

6

True. Japan has received about 76 metres of snow this century. That's about as high as a 25-storey building!

7

b. There are thunderstorms over Lake Maracaibo on 260–300 nights per year, with an average of 28 lightning strikes per minute for up to 10 hours at a time in peak lightning season. The lake is hit by lightning up to 40,000 times in one night.

8

c. So much charge going down such a narrow channel generates a temperature of 30,000 °C—five times hotter than the surface of the Sun.

9

a. Antarctica is even colder than the Arctic because it is a mountainous land mass rather than a stretch of sea ice. The higher you go, the colder it gets.

10

c. The USA, on average, can witness over 1000 tornadoes a year.

CONTINENTS

1

A continent is a very large area of land. How many continents are there in the world?

a. 4
b. 7
c. 13

2

Which of these is NOT a continent?

North America
South America
Europe
Asia
Africa
Australasia
The Arctic
Antarctica

3

The largest continent is North America.
True or false?

4

How many countries are there in Africa?

a. 4
b. 24
c. 54

5

Which country owns Antarctica?

a. No country
b. South Africa
c. Britain

6

The country of Russia lies in 2 continents.
True or false?

7

Europe is the world's second-smallest continent. How much of the world's population lives there?

a. One tenth
b. One seventh
c. One quarter

DID YOU KNOW?

Greenland, the planet's largest island, is in the continent of North America, but it actually belongs to Denmark, located in Europe.

8

What famous waterway separates North America from South America?

a. The Panama Canal

b. The Suez Canal

c. The Manchester Ship Canal

9

Most of the world's continents used to be joined together in a 'super-continent' called Pangea.

True or false?

10

Which continent has the world's largest coral reef?

a. Asia

b. Australasia

c. Antarctica

CONTINENTS

1

b.
There are
7 continents
in the world.

2

The Arctic.
The 7 continents
are North America,
South America,
Europe, Asia, Africa,
Australasia and
Antarctica.

3

False.
Asia is the
largest
continent;
Australasia is
the smallest.

4

c.
Africa has
54 countries
– the most
countries of any
continent.

5

a.
No country owns
Antarctica and no
one lives there, but
scientists from many
different countries
visit to do research.

6

True.
Most of Russia
is in Asia, but
part of it is
in Europe,
including
its capital,
Moscow.

7

c.
Europe is
made up of
44 countries.

8

a.

This 82 km (51 mile) waterway – The Panama Canal (above) – connects the Pacific and Atlantic oceans.

9

True.

From about 280 to 230 million years ago, Pangea was a 'super-continent' that joined many of today's individual continents.

10

b.

Australasia is home to the Great Barrier Reef, which is the only living thing that is visible from space!

OCEANS

1 **What is the world's largest ocean?**
a. Atlantic Ocean
b. Pacific Ocean
c. Southern Ocean

2 **How much of our planet's surface is covered with seawater?**
a. 33%
b. 50%
c. 70%

3 **What is the Mariana Trench?**
a. The deepest feature on Earth
b. A coat worn by mermaids
c. A type of fish

4 **The Earth's longest mountain range lies under the ocean.**
True or false?

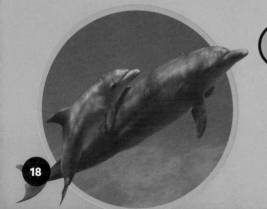

5 **Approximately how many known species live in the ocean?**
a. 4600
b. 46,000
c. 460,000

6 **What is a main cause of sea level rise?**
a. Melting glaciers and ice sheets
b. An increase in rainfall
c. The number of shipwrecks at
   the bottom of the ocean

7 **Does the Atlantic Ocean...**
a. Get wider every year?
b. Stay the same width?
c. Get narrower every year?

8 **Which ocean current in the North Atlantic brings warm weather to Europe?**
a. The Gull Stream   b. The Gulf Stream   c. The Golf Stream

9 **The world has 10 named oceans.**
True or false?

10 **If you placed Mount Everest at the deepest part of the ocean, the top of it would stick up out of the water.**
True or false?

OCEANS

1 **b.** The Pacific Ocean covers a third of Earth's surface and holds over half of all its water.

2 **c.** Around 70% of our planet is open ocean.

3 **a.** The trench is under the Pacific Ocean. The deepest point is called the Challenger Deep.

4 **True.** There is a mid-ocean ridge that runs continuously through all the world's oceans. It is almost 10 times longer than the Andes, the longest mountain range on land.

5 **c.** But so much of the ocean is unexplored that scientists think there could be over 2 million species of life under the surface.

6 **a.** World sea level has changed a lot in the Earth's history, depending on how much ice there is on land and what the temperature of the sea is.

7 **a.** The tectonic plates that Europe and North America sit on are drifting apart – but very slowly. The Atlantic widens by around 2 cm every year.

8 **b.** The Gulf Stream brings warm weather to Europe.

9 **False.** There are 5 named modern oceans: the Atlantic, Pacific, Indian, Arctic and Southern.

10 **False.** It would be completely swallowed up. The deepest known point in the Earth's seabed is about 10,900 m deep and Mount Everest is 8848 m tall, so the peak would be *under* water.

EARTHQUAKES

1 **Who is most likely to study earthquakes?**
a. A landscaper   b. A seismologist   c. An earthquakologist

2 **The boundary where tectonic plates meet is called what?**
a. Fault line
b. Crunch line
c. Washing line

3 **Earthquakes happen when tectonic plates push against each other, causing tension to build up. This causes waves of energy to be released. What are these waves called?**
a. Sonic waves
b. Mexican waves
c. Seismic waves

4 **Earthquakes are happening more often.**
True or false?

5 **The power of earthquakes is measured on what scale?**
a. Von Richthofen scale
b. Richter scale
c. Von Trapp scale

DID YOU KNOW?
The British Geological Survey records an earthquake nearly every day, but they are usually too weak to be felt by anyone.

6 An earthquake under the ocean can cause which type of wave?
a. Tidal wave
b. Tsunami
c. Barrel wave

7 What was the most powerful earthquake ever recorded?
a. San Francisco earthquake of 1906
b. Chilean earthquake of 1960
c. Sumatra earthquake of 2004

8 What is the epicentre of an earthquake?
a. The place deep in the Earth where the earthquake starts
b. The spot on the Earth's surface directly over the earthquake's centre
c. The middle point in a tsunami wave

9 About 90% of the world's earthquakes occur around which ocean?
a. Pacific Ocean   b. Atlantic Ocean   c. Indian Ocean

10 What are children in Japan trained to do when an earthquake hits?
a. Run outside and climb the nearest tree
b. Phone a special earthquake hotline
c. Shelter under their desks

EARTHQUAKES

1 **b.** Seismologists study all things earthquake-related.

2 **a.** Fault line.

3 **c.** It's this sudden release of energy as seismic waves that causes earthquakes.

4 **False.** There is no evidence that earthquakes are on the increase.

5 **b.** The Richter scale was invented by an American seismologist called Charles Richter in 1935.

6 **b.** Earthquakes can cause giant waves known as tsunamis.

7 **b.** The Chilean earthquake of 1960 measured 9.5 on the Richter scale. Its tsunami created waves that travelled thousands of kilometres.

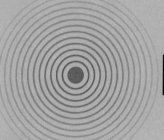

8 **b.** The epicentre of an earthquake is usually where the most damage occurs.

9 **a.** Most of the world's earthquakes happen in the Pacific Ocean, which is known as the 'Ring of Fire'.

10 **c.** Sheltering under your school desk is a way to protect yourself if an earthquake hits.

1 Canada is the largest country in the world.

2 Russia is so large it has 7 different time zones.

3 On a map, Spain is shaped like a boot.

4 Monaco is the smallest country in the world.

5 Thailand used to be called Siam.

6 South Sudan is the world's newest country.

7 The official language of Brazil is Spanish.

8 The 'Democratic People's Republic of Korea' is the longest country name in the world.

9 You could fit the UK into Australia 20 times over.

10 Most of the Amazon Rainforest lies in Argentina.

DID YOU KNOW?
Australia is the largest country without land borders, and is also the largest country in the southern hemisphere.

27

DID YOU KNOW?

Saint Basil's Cathedral in Moscow wasn't always this brightly coloured – originally it was said to be white.

1

FALSE.
Canada is the second largest country with an area of almost 10 million km². Russia is the largest at over 17 million km².

2

FALSE.
Russia has 11 different time zones.

3

FALSE.
Italy is shaped like a boot.

4

FALSE.
The Vatican City is the smallest country in the world.

5

TRUE.
It has been known as Thailand since 1948.

6

TRUE.
South Sudan declared independence in 2011, making it the newest country in the world.

7

FALSE.
Brazil's official language is actually Portuguese.

8

FALSE.
The longest country name in the world is actually 'The United Kingdom of Great Britain and Northern Ireland'. No wonder it is shortened to 'the UK'!

9

FALSE.
You could, in fact, fit the UK into Australia almost 32 times over!

10

FALSE.
The Amazon Rainforest is mostly in Brazil.

MOUNTAIN RANGES

TRUE or **FALSE**

1

Mountain peaks in Scotland measuring over 3000 feet (or 914.4 metres) are known as Munros.

2

The Himalayas are spread across three different countries.

3

At 8848 metres, Mount Everest is the tallest mountain in the world.

4

The Matterhorn is a mountain in the Alps that is shaped like a square-based pyramid.

5

Table Mountain in South Africa is shaped like a table.

6

The Snowy Mountains are a range of mountains in Australia, but it is too hot to ever actually snow on them.

7

The Andes in South America is the world's longest mountain range on land.

8

The Caucasus mountain range has the highest mountains in Europe.

9

There is a mountain range in New Zealand called The Incredibles.

10

At 1085 metres, Snowdon is the highest mountain in Britain.

DID YOU KNOW?

There are officially 6 different routes up Snowdon, and there is also a train to the summit if you don't want to walk.

MOUNTAIN RANGES

TRUE or FALSE

DID YOU KNOW?

Alpacas can be found high in the Andes mountain range and are descended from the camel family. They are a domesticated version of the vicuña.

QUIZ 7 ANSWERS

1

TRUE.
Munros are named after Sir Hugh Munro who created a table in 1891 of Scotland's highest summits.

2

FALSE.
The Himalayas are spread across Bhutan, China, India, Nepal, Afghanistan and Pakistan.

3

TRUE.
Mount Everest is over 200 metres taller than the second tallest mountain – K2 – which is 8611 metres high.

4

TRUE.
Each of the Matterhorn's four sides align with the compass points – north, south, east and west.

5

TRUE.
Its flat top really does make it look like a table!

6

FALSE.
The Snowy Mountains are well named!

7

TRUE.
The Andes are about 7000 km long.

8

TRUE.
There are six peaks in the Caucasus that are higher than any of the Alps. Mount Elbrus at 5642 metres is the highest mountain in Europe.

9

FALSE.
The mountain range is actually called The Remarkables. This is because they look spectacular.

10

FALSE.
Ben Nevis is the highest mountain in Britain. It is 1345 metres tall.

RIVERS

1

Streams and small rivers often flow into big rivers. What are these small feeder rivers called?

a. Little rivers

b. Meanders

c. Tributaries

2

The longest river in the world is 6650 km long—what is its name?

a. Nile

b. Amazon

c. Mississippi

3

How long did it take the author David Walliams to swim the length of the Thames?

a. 8 hours

b. 8 days

c. 8 weeks

4

The Amazon, Ganges and Indus rivers all share an unusual creature that lives in their waters. What is it?

a. Duck-billed platypus

b. Dwarf hippopotamus

c. Dolphin

5

There are no bridges across the Amazon River.

True or false?

6

What is the world's deepest river?

a. Amazon

b. Congo

c. Thames

7

How many countries does the River Danube flow through?

a. 1

b. 5

c. 10

8

Starting in 2008, a man named Ed Stafford walked the entire length of the Amazon river! How long did it take him?

a. 2 days

b. 2 months

c. Over 2 years

9

Rivers are so powerful they can cut valleys through the rock. The Colorado River carved this valley on the left. What is its name?

a. The Marianas Trench

b. The Grand Canyon

c. The Panama Cut

10

Caño Cristales – 'The River of Five Colours' – in Colombia has flowing water that is bright blue, red, black, yellow and green.

True or false?

RIVERS

1

c.
Small feeder rivers are called tributaries. Meanders are when a river flows in a series of large sweeping curves.

2

a.
The Nile is the longest river in the world. The Amazon is second longest at 6575 km and the Yangtze is the third longest at 6380 km.

3

b.
David swam 225 km from the source in Gloucestershire to Westminster Bridge in London in 2011, raising over £1 million for charity.

4

c.
There are 6 species of dolphin that live in the world's freshwater rivers.

5

True.
No bridges span the width of the Amazon river. Local ferries are used to carry people and goods across.

6

b.

The Congo's true depth remains a mystery, but it is at least 220 m deep in some places. You could stack two-and-a-half Big Ben clock towers on top of each other, drop them in, and they'd still disappear beneath the surface!

7

c.

The Danube flows through Germany, Austria, Slovakia, Hungary, Croatia, Serbia, Romania, Bulgaria, Moldova and Ukraine.

8

c.

Ed Stafford's hike took 860 days—almost two and a half years!

9

b.

The Grand Canyon is up to 29 km wide and 1857 m deep.

10

True.

Because of the aquatic plants in the river, it looks multicoloured!

CAPITAL CITIES

Can you match the capital city with the correct country?
And then match it to the correct photo?

City	Country
Rome	France
Tokyo	Russia
Copenhagen	England
Washington, DC	Greece
Delhi	Scotland
Athens	Denmark
Edinburgh	Italy
London	USA
Moscow	Japan
Paris	India

1

2

3

4

5

6

7

8

9

10

CAPITAL CITIES

1

Washington, DC, USA

2

Athens, Greece

3

Moscow, Russia

4

Delhi, India

5

Copenhagen, Denmark

6

London, England

7

Tokyo, Japan

8

Paris, France

9

Rome, Italy

10

Edinburgh, Scotland

SHIPS AND BOATS

1 What type of vehicles race in the America's Cup?

a. Surfboards

b. Sailing yachts

c. Steam ships

2 The first kayaks were made by stretching animal skins over a frame of wood or whale bones.

True or false?

3 Norwegian explorer Thor Heyerdahl crossed the Pacific Ocean on what kind of vessel?

a. Raft

b. Jet-ski

c. Rowing boat

4 A slow-moving boat used to carry cargo and passengers on canals is called what?

a. Barge

b. Canoe

c. Snail

5 What were the fastest-ever commercial sailing vessels called?

a. Tea clippers

b. Coffee flyers

c. Cocoa slippers

6 *Titanic* was the largest ship in the world when it launched. It sank when it hit a rocky reef.

True or false?

7 Which sea vessel is most likely to have a periscope?

a. A jet-ski

b. A sea kayak

c. A submarine

8 The wreck of the *Mary Rose* was raised from the sea in 1982. Which king of England did she belong to?

a. William the Conqueror

b. Alfred the Great

c. Henry VIII

9 What did the boat *Spirit of Australia* do in 1978 that made it famous?

a. It was the first yacht to sail all the way around Australia.

b. It set a new water speed record.

c. It sailed from Southampton to Sydney in a record 39 days.

10 Which of these is a type of ship from China?

a. A junk

b. A rubbish

c. A garbage

43

SHIPS AND BOATS

1

b. The America's Cup competition began in 1851 as a race around the Isle of Wight in England.

2

True. The first kayaks were made over 4000 years ago.

3

a. The raft, called the *Kon-Tiki*, had a bamboo cabin big enough for the crew of six!

4

a. Barge.

5
a. Tea clippers were designed in the 19th century to carry tea from China to England as fast as possible.

6
False. *Titanic* sank after hitting an iceberg in the North Atlantic Ocean.

7
c. Periscopes let submarines look above the surface of the water while remaining underwater.

8
c. She belonged to Henry VIII and sank off the south coast of England in 1545. She lay underwater for over 400 years.

9
b. *Spirit of Australia* set a water speed record of 511 km/h. The record is one of the most dangerous in the world to beat. No wonder it has stood for over 40 years!

10
a. Junk ships are Chinese sailing ships with huge sails.

AIRCRAFT AND AIRPORTS

1 The first flight of a powered aircraft was in 1903. Who made the flight?

a. The Wright brothers   b. The Flying sisters   c. The Right crew

2 Amelia Earhart set lots of aviation records. Which bird was her yellow plane named after?

a. A goldfinch   b. A yellowhammer   c. A canary

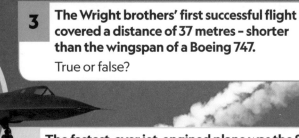

3 The Wright brothers' first successful flight covered a distance of 37 metres – shorter than the wingspan of a Boeing 747.

True or false?

4 The fastest-ever jet-engined plane was the SR-71 spy plane, which could travel over three times the speed of sound. What was the plane's nickname?

a. Blackbird   b. Tomcat   c. Desert Eagle

5 The biggest airport in the world is Heathrow in England.

True or false?

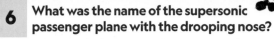

6 What was the name of the supersonic passenger plane with the drooping nose?

a. Ripcord   b. Concorde   c. Zipcord

7 Helicopters are used to fight fires by carrying tanks or buckets full of water.

True or false?

8 The Antonov An-225 is the world's largest cargo plane. How many African elephants could it carry at once?

a. 10   b. 25   c. 50

9 What is the code for Gatwick airport near London?

a. GAT   b. LGW   c. LON

10 What is unusual about landing at the airport on the Isle of Barra in the Outer Hebrides, Scotland?

a. You land on the beach.

b. You land in a forest.

c. You have to wear aviator goggles.

AIRCRAFT AND AIRPORTS

1 **a.** The Wright brothers made their historic flight in North Carolina, USA.

2 **c.** *Canary* was the first plane that Amelia Earhart owned.

3 **True.** The Wright brothers' first successful flight only lasted 12 seconds.

4 **a.** This record-breaking plane was painted black as camouflage against the night sky. That's how it got its name.

5 **False.** King Fahd International Airport in Dammam, Saudi Arabia is the largest airport in the world, covering 776 km².

6 **b.** Concorde could fly from New York to London in less than 3 hours.

7 **True.** They are regularly used to fight fires in forests and bushland in the USA and Australia.

8 **c.** The Antonov An-225 cargo plane could carry 50 African elephants.

9 **b.** LGW stands for London Gatwick.

10 **a.** Barra's runway is on the beach!

NATIONAL FLAGS

Can you match the flags with the countries they represent?

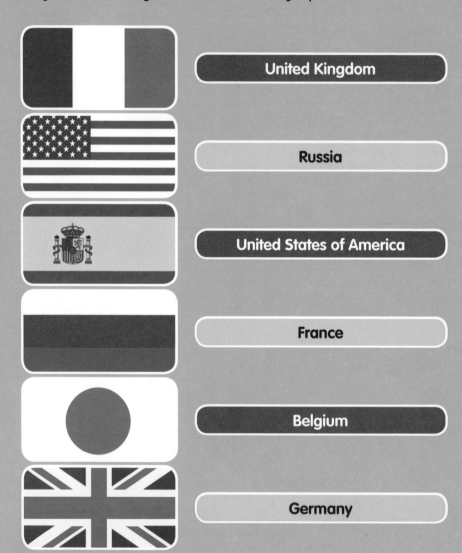

United Kingdom

Russia

United States of America

France

Belgium

Germany

Australia

New Zealand

Japan

Nepal

Spain

Canada

NATIONAL FLAGS

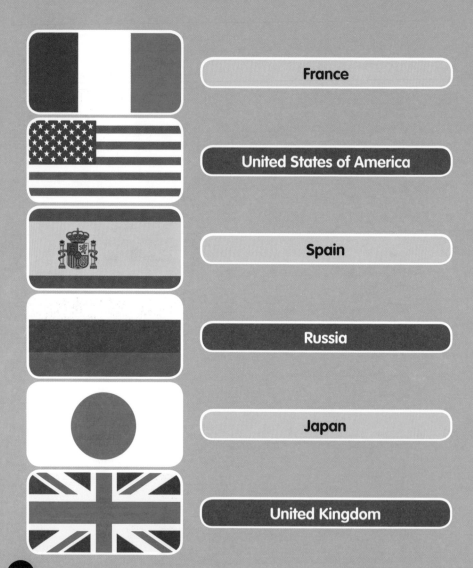

France

United States of America

Spain

Russia

Japan

United Kingdom

New Zealand

Australia

Canada

Germany

Nepal

Belgium

ABANDONED PLACES

1

The town of Pripyat in Ukraine was completely abandoned on 27 April 1986. Why?

a. It was flooded when a nearby dam burst.

b. It was a gold mining town and all the gold was dug out of the mine.

c. There was an explosion at the nearby nuclear power plant.

2

Hashima is an abandoned coal mining island in Japan. Which James Bond film did it feature in?

a. Skyfall

b. Dr No

c. The Spy Who Loved Me

3

Aldwych underground station closed to the public in 1994. It was located in central Manchester.

True or false?

4

Why was the Scottish island of St Kilda (pictured below) abandoned in 1930?

a. It was on a volcano.

b. The island was attacked by pirates.

c. Life there had become too difficult.

5

The village of Imber in England was abandoned during World War II. Why?

a. A huge bomb fell on the church but didn't explode.

b. It was used as a training village by troops.

c. It was invaded by the German army.

6

There is a famous Inca city in Peru that was abandoned over 400 years ago. What is it called?

a. Machu Picchu

b. Pretoria

c. Pikachu

7

Why was a theme park in New Orleans, USA, abandoned in 2005?

a. Its rides were too scary.

b. It was damaged by a hurricane.

c. It ran out of hot dogs.

8

Below is an abandoned Olympic sporting venue. What sport did athletes once compete at here to win gold?

a. BMX freestyle

b. Shooting

c. Ski jumping

9

In 1872, the *Mary Celeste* was found drifting in the Atlantic. It was in good condition but had been completely abandoned by its crew and passengers, who were never seen again.

True or false?

10

Poveglia is an abandoned island near Venice. What did Poveglia used to be?

a. A customs check point

b. A quarantine station for plague victims

c. A hospital for people with mental illnesses

55

ABANDONED PLACES

1

c.

Pripyat, Ukraine was built to serve the Chernobyl nuclear power plant, which suffered a devastating accident.

2

a.

Hashima was the setting for the villain's secret base.

3

False.

Aldwych was a tube station in central London. There were plans for the line that Aldwych is on to be extended, but this never happened and it was closed in 1994.

4

c.

The 36 inhabitants voted to leave the island and move to the Scottish mainland.

5

b.

American troops trained in Imber before the D-Day invasion of 1944.

6

a.

This amazing citadel of Machu Picchu perches on a 2430 m high mountain ridge.

7

b.
It was seriously damaged by flooding caused by Hurricane Katrina.

8

c.
This was the ski jump at Cortina d'Ampezzo in Italy, which held the Winter Olympics in 1956.

9

True.
No one has ever explained the mystery of what happened to the crew of the *Mary Celeste*.

10

a, b and c.
Poveglia has had many interesting roles, but it has been abandoned since the hospital closed in 1968.

WORLD WONDERS

1

There were Seven Wonders of the Ancient World, but only one still exists today. Which one?

a. The Colossus of Rhodes

b. The Great Pyramid of Giza

c. The Hanging Gardens of Babylon

2

The Lighthouse of Alexandria in Egypt was one of the tallest buildings in the world for many centuries. How was it destroyed?

a. It was burnt down by the Romans.

b. A huge ship crashed into it.

c. It was flattened by earthquakes.

3

In 2007, a set of New Seven Wonders of the World were announced. How were they chosen?

a. By a lottery

b. By a public vote

c. By whoever paid the most money

4

The Taj Mahal was completed in 1653. What purpose was it built for?

a. Temple

b. Tomb

c. Theatre

5

From this list of 12 present-day wonders, can you select the 7 that were chosen?

1) Stonehenge, England

2) Great Pyramid of Giza, Egypt

3) Colosseum, Rome

4) Panama Canal, Panama

5) Great Wall of China, China

6) Christ the Redeemer, Brazil

7) Chichen Itza, Mexico

8) Palace of Versailles, France

9) Taj Mahal, India

10) Petra, Jordan

11) Burj Khalifa, Dubai

12) Machu Picchu, Peru

6

The statue of Christ the Redeemer stands above which Brazilian city?

a. São Paulo

b. Rio de Janeiro

c. Brasília

7

The Great Wall of China can be seen from space?

True or false?

8

Why is Petra in Jordan known as the 'Rose City'?

a. It was built from rose-coloured stone.

b. It was named after a lady called Rose.

c. Many roses are grown there.

9

Chichen Itza is a large Mayan city. What was this stone feature used for?

a. It was used for tying up llamas.

b. Warriors used it to do chin-ups to show their strength.

c. It was a hoop used in an ancient ballgame.

10

The Colosseum in Rome was the largest amphitheatre in the world when it was completed in 80 AD. What did people go there to see?

a. Gladiator fights

b. Drama

c. Mock sea battles

WORLD WONDERS

1

b.

The Great Pyramid is still standing in Egypt. All the other ancient wonders have been destroyed.

2

c.

After two earthquakes damaged the Lighthouse of Alexandria, a third one finally toppled it in the 14th century.

3

b.

The New Seven Wonders of the World were chosen in 2007 by a public vote.

4

b.

The Taj Mahal was built by the Mughal Emperor Shah Jahan in memory of his beloved late wife, Mumtaz Mahal.

5

The 7 present-day wonders are:

Colosseum, Rome

Petra, Jordan

Great Wall of China, China

Christ the Redeemer, Brazil

Chichen Itza, Mexico

Taj Mahal, India

Machu Picchu, Peru

6

b.
The Christ the Redeemer statue stands high on a rock looking down over the city.

7

False.
The wall cannot be seen with the naked eye from space.

8

a.
Petra is the Greek word for stone.

DID YOU KNOW?

The Colosseum in Rome is so big that it had 80 entrances and could easily fit a football pitch inside.

9

c.
Chichen Itza has several ball courts where an ancient ballgame was played. The largest court was bigger than a football pitch.

10

a, b and c.
Around 50,000 spectators came to watch gladiator fights, dramas and even mock sea battles at the Colosseum (below), as the arena could be flooded with water.

WATERFALLS

1
Angel Falls, the tallest waterfall in the world, was discovered in 1933.

2
Angel Falls is taller than the highest mountain in England.

3
Niagara Falls is found in Nigeria.

4
The picture opposite shows Rainbow Falls.

5
Victoria Falls is named after Victoria Beckham.

6
Waterfalls can't freeze, because the water in them is always moving.

7
At 177 m tall, Cautley Spout is the highest waterfall in the UK.

8
The picture below shows an underwater waterfall.

9
There is a waterfall in Hawaii that flows upwards.

10
One theory says that the Mediterranean Sea was created by a colossal waterfall.

WATERFALLS

1

TRUE.
Angel Falls was first made known to the outside world by a pilot called Jimmie Angel who first flew over it in 1933.

2

TRUE.
Angel Falls is taller by a metre! It is 979 metres high but England's highest mountain, Scafell Pike, is 978 metres high.

3

FALSE.
Niagara Falls spans the border between Ontario in Canada and the state of New York in the US.

4

FALSE.
The picture shows Victoria Falls on the Zambezi river in southern Africa.

5

FALSE.
It is named after Queen Victoria who was the ruler of Britain when David Livingstone, the Scottish missionary and explorer, became the first European to view Victoria Falls in 1855.

6

FALSE.
If the temperature of the water becomes cold enough, the water flowing into the waterfall will slow down and eventually freeze.

7

FALSE.
Cautley Spout is the highest waterfall in England. The highest in the UK is Eas a' Chul Aluinn in Scotland at 201 m tall.

9

TRUE.
In wet and windy conditions, the well-named Upside Down Falls in Hawaii only cascades downwards for a few metres before being blown back uphill.

10

TRUE.
The Mediterranean was a dry basin 5.3 million years ago, with Africa and Spain joined together. It is thought that Africa and Spain then moved apart and the waters of the Atlantic Ocean poured in to create a new sea.

8

FALSE.
It's actually an optical illusion showing sand from a Mauritius beach being swept off a shallow coastal shelf into a deeper part of the ocean by currents.

TRADITIONS AND CELEBRATIONS

1   **Guy Fawkes Night is celebrated with fireworks and bonfires on 5 November. What does it celebrate?**
a. The birth of a famous Prime Minister
b. Foiling a plot to blow up Parliament
c. The anniversary of the Great Fire of London

2   **During the festival of Chinese New Year, children are traditionally given red envelopes. What is inside the envelopes?**
a. Money   b. A shopping list   c. Extra homework

3   **Hanukkah is a Jewish festival that happens in November or December. How long does it last for?**
a. A weekend   b. 4 days and 4 nights   c. 8 days and 8 nights

4   **In the song '12 Days of Christmas', what did my true love bring on the third day of Christmas?**
a. 3 turtle doves
b. 3 swans a-swimming
c. 3 French hens

5   **Eid al-Fitr is a Muslim festival. What does 'Eid al-Fitr' mean?**
a. Festival of breaking the fast
b. Festival of the new year
c. Festival of the harvest

6 On New Year's Eve, people often make a promise that they will try to do something in the coming year. What is this promise called?

a. New Year's goal

b. New Year's resolution

c. New Year's evolution

 7 When do Americans celebrate Independence Day?

a. 4 July

b. 14 July

c. 25 December

 8 What does the name 'Halloween' mean?

a. Greetings to Ian

b. The evening before All Hallows' Day

c. Festival of witches

 9 Which country celebrates St Patrick's Day?

a. Iceland   b. Scotland   c. Ireland

 10 People send romantic cards and gifts on 14 February. Who is this tradition named after?

a. Saint Valentine

b. Saint Romantine

c. Saint Clementine

TRADITIONS AND CELEBRATIONS

1

b.

Guy Fawkes plotted to blow up King James I and Parliament in 1605.

2

a.

The envelopes are red because that is a lucky colour in China.

3

c.

Hanukkah celebrations last for 8 days and 8 nights and include lighting candles, playing games and eating special foods.

4

c.

3 French hens – there were 2 turtle doves and 7 swans a-swimming.

5

a.

The three-day festival marks the end of the fasting month of Ramadan. The date varies each year according to the phases of the moon.

6

b.
Some New Year's resolutions last longer than others!

7

a.
Independence Day is a celebration of the day the original 13 colonies became one new country.

8

b.
All Hallows' Day is on 1 November, the day after Halloween, and is a day when Christians honour their saints.

9

c.
Saint Patrick is the patron saint of Ireland, although this day is now celebrated in many countries worldwide.

10

a.
Saint Valentine was executed by the Romans on 14 February. Legend says that on the morning of that day he gave a note of thanks to a girl. He signed it, 'Your Valentine'.

DID YOU KNOW?
It's thought that eating crickets could help improve the health of your digestive system!

2

There is a restaurant in Wales where you can eat bug burgers, cricket kebabs and bamboo worm fudge ice cream.

3

The largest circular pizza ever cooked was as heavy as a car.

1

Tarantula spiders are a delicacy in Cambodia.

5

Squid ink is a popular pizza topping in Japan.

6

Paella is an Italian pasta dish.

4

Truffles are a rare delicacy that grow in forests and are collected using pigs to sniff them out.

8

Humans cannot eat dog food.

9

Gazpacho soup is unusual because you eat it cold.

7

Haggis is made using the meat of a chubby rodent that lives wild in the Scottish Highlands.

10

The United Kingdom eats more baked beans than all the other countries in the world combined.

FOOD

1

TRUE.
Tarantulas are usually fried.

2

TRUE.
Grub Kitchen was Britain's first insect restaurant and it opened in 2015.

3

FALSE.
The largest circular pizza ever cooked weighed as much as a double-decker bus!

DID YOU KNOW?

Fried tarantulas are said to taste like a cross between chicken and cod, but have a much crispier texture on the outside.

72

5

TRUE.
The black ink tastes rather salty and makes the pizza look burnt!

6

FALSE.
Paella is a Spanish rice dish.

4

TRUE.
Pigs are naturally good at rooting around for food – including truffles – with their snouts. The only problem is stopping the pigs eating the truffles when they find them!

7

FALSE.
Haggis is made from a sheep's heart, liver and lungs minced with oatmeal and spices, and is traditionally cooked in the animal's stomach.

8

FALSE.
Dog food is perfectly edible. There are even people whose job it is to taste pet food to make sure it is up to standard.

9

TRUE.
Gazpacho is made of raw blended ingredients like tomatoes, peppers and cucumbers. It is very popular in summer as it is cool and refreshing.

10

TRUE.
1.5 million cans of Heinz baked beans are sold every day in the UK.

AMAZING JOURNEYS

1

What did Captain Tom Moore set out to do in the days before his 100th birthday in 2020?

a. Walk on his hands for 100 steps

b. Climb the stairs 100 times

c. Walk 100 laps of his garden

2

Dmitri Galitzine crossed the Solent between England and the Isle of Wight in just under 2 hours. The boat he used was made from a motor fitted to a what?

a. Wheelbarrow

b. Inflatable crocodile

c. Pumpkin

3

What did Ross Edgley take 157 days to do in 2018?

a. Swim around the whole of the UK mainland

b. Climb every mountain in the UK over 500 m high

c. Pedal from Land's End to John o'Groats on a unicycle

4

What unusual journey did Phyllis Pearsall complete in 1936?

a. Swimming the length of the Thames

b. Walking along every street in London

c. Walking backwards from Edinburgh to London

5

What was unusual about the way Mick Cullen walked from John o'Groats to Land's End in the winter of 2019–2020?

a. He walked backwards.

b. He wore just his swimming trunks.

c. He walked blindfolded.

6

Charles Darwin spent five years circumnavigating the world, studying plants and animals. What was the name of his ship?

a. HMS *Beagle*

b. HMS *Snoopy*

c. HMS *Woodstock*

7

Which two cities are connected in the longest continuous train journey in the world?

a. Moscow and St Petersburg

b. Moscow and Pyongyang

c. London and Barcelona

8

Who was the first person to walk on the Moon?

a. Neil Armstrong

b. Buzz Aldrin

c. Buzz Lightyear

9

In the 18th century, a British naval captain (left) made the first recorded circumnavigation of New Zealand on HMS *Endeavour*. What was his name?

a. Ernest Shackleton

b. James Cook

c. Jack Sparrow

10

What amazing thing did Amelia Earhart do in 1932 that made her famous?

a. She became the first woman to fly a plane.

b. She became the first woman to fly solo across the Atlantic Ocean.

c. She became the first woman to fly a helicopter.

AMAZING JOURNEYS

1

c.
Captain Tom raised over £32 million for the NHS during the coronavirus pandemic.

2

c.
Dmitri got his 360 kg pumpkin from a giant vegetable show.

3

a.
Ross (below) swam 2882 km around the entire UK mainland and was stung by jellyfish 37 times.

4

b.
Phyllis walked over 4800 km to check the names of London's 23,000 streets for an A–Z map of the city that she published.

5

b.
'Speedo' Mick raised more than £300,000 for charity.

6

a.
Darwin observed hundreds of different species in many different countries.

7

b.
The journey between Moscow and Pyongyang takes eight days.

8

a.
The Apollo 11 space mission went to the Moon in 1969.

9

b.
Cook made several voyages, exploring thousands of miles of previously unknown areas of the globe.

10

b.
Earhart (below) set many other amazing aviation records as well as being the first woman to fly solo across the Atlantic Ocean.

HAMMOND·Y

DEPARTMENT OF

BUREAU OF

1 **Where is the tallest building in the world?**
a. London   b. Dubai   c. New York

2 **Which is the world's most-visited museum?**
a. Harry Potter Museum, UK
b. The British Lawnmower Museum, UK
c. The Louvre, France

3 **The Sagrada Familia is a famous basilica being built in Barcelona. How long has it been under construction for?**
a. 38 years   b. 138 years   c. 1380 years

4 **What building material are igloos made out of?**
a. Glass   b. Snow   c. Reeds

5 **The Empire State Building was the first building to have more than 100 floors.** True or false?

6 **What is this famous building on the right?**
a. Pompidou Centre
b. Madison Square Garden
c. Sydney Opera House

7 **What is the function of the very unusual building opposite?**
a. School   b. Library   c. Psychiatric hospital

8 **The US Department of Defense has its home in the world's largest office building. What is this building called?**
a. The Octagon   b. The Drill Square   c. The Pentagon

9 **What is so unusual about the Great Mosque of Djenné in West Africa?**
a. It is the largest mud-brick building in the world.
b. It was built upside-down.
c. It is completely underground.

10 **Which of these is NOT a real building in London?**
a. The Gherkin   b. The Walkie-Talkie   c. The Cream Tea

DID YOU KNOW?

If you were to walk a lap around the outside of the Pentagon, you would cover around 1.4 km.

1 **b.** At 830 m, the Burj Khalifa has held the record for the tallest building since 2010.

2 **c.** 9.6 million people a year visit the Louvre in Paris to see the painting of the Mona Lisa.

3 **b.** Construction of the Sagrada Familia began in 1882. The basilica should be finished by 2026.

4 **b.** Igloos, made of snow, are surprisingly warm inside and can be large – some can house 20 people.

5 **True.** The Empire State Building was completed in 1931 and was the tallest building in the world for 40 years.

6 **c.** This famous symbol of Australia – the Sydney Opera House – was completed in 1973.

7 **b.** This mind-boggling library in Nice, France, is called 'La Tête Carrée' which means 'The Square Head'.

8 **c.** The Pentagon has five sides, five floors above ground, and five ring corridors per floor with a total of 28.2 km of corridors.

9 **a.** The Great Mosque's mud and plaster walls are repaired annually by the local people to protect the building from erosion.

10 **c.** The Gherkin (left) and the Walkie-Talkie are fitting nicknames for two unusual-looking buildings; however, the Cream Tea is not a building in London.

DESERTS

1

What is the name of the world's largest desert?

a. Sahara

b. Antarctica

c. Australian

2

How much of Earth's land surface is desert?

a. 3%

b. 13%

c. 33%

3

The Atacama is the driest desert in the world. For how long did some some parts go without any rain at all?

a. 40 months

b. 4 years

c. 500 years

4

What is the name for a place in a desert where water comes up from deep underground?

a. A sanctuary

b. An oasis

c. A blur

5

In very hot places, people sometimes think they can see a pool of water which isn't really there. What is this called?

a. A mirage

b. A mirror

c. A minion

6

All deserts are hot.
True or false?

7

Camels have adapted well to living in deserts. What do they store in their humps?

a. Water
b. Fat
c. Chocolate

8

How many times could you fit the United Kingdom into the Sahara Desert?

a. 8
b. 38
c. 88

9

Many deserts have sand dunes. How tall are the world's highest sand dunes? Almost as tall as...

a. A giraffe
b. The Eiffel Tower
c. Ben Nevis

10

Which of these is NOT a desert?

a. Gobi
b. Kalahari
c. Mari

DESERTS

1

b.

Deserts are the driest places on Earth, but they aren't always hot and sandy. Both the Arctic and Antarctica are deserts because they get very little precipitation.

2

c.

One third of Earth's land is arid or semi-arid, making it desert.

3

c.

There is evidence that for 500 years before 2015, no rain at all fell in parts of the Atacama desert.

4

b.

Some oases are said to hold water that fell as rain 20,000 years ago.

5

a.

A mirage is an optical illusion caused when hot air interacts with the light from the sky.

6

False.

Some deserts are cold, like Antarctica—they're classed as deserts due to the fact that they receive very little precipitation.

7

b.

Camels' humps are a reserve of fat, not water.

8

b.

If the Sahara Desert were a country, it would be the fifth biggest country in the world.

9

c.

There is a dune 1230 m high in Argentina. Ben Nevis is 1345 m high and is the tallest mountain in the UK.

10

c.

The Gobi is a cold desert in Asia and the Kalahari is a hot desert in southern Africa.

ISLANDS

1

What is the largest island in the world?
a. Australia
b. Greenland
c. The Isle of Wight

2

What is the name of the island that Scotland, England and Wales occupy?
a. Ireland
b. The United Kingdom
c. Great Britain

3

Which islands in the Indian Ocean are in danger of disappearing?
a. The Maldives
b. The Saldives
c. The Indianos

4

On which island can you see these carved moai statues?
a. Christmas Island
b. Easter Island
c. Halloween Island

5

Hawaii is the only US state made up of islands.
True or false?

6

What is a collection of islands called?

a. Archipelago

b. Shoal

c. Flock

7

What is the largest artificial island in the world?

a. The Flevopolder, the Netherlands

b. The island built for Kansai International Airport, Japan

c. Palm Jumeirah, Dubai

8

Which country has the most islands?

a. Norway

b. Canada

c. Philippines

9

The island of East Island disappeared in 2018 when a volcano blew it apart.

True or false?

10

What is special about the island called Vulcan Point in the Philippines (below)?

a. It has the most volcanoes of any island.

b. It is an island in a lake on an island in a lake on an island.

c. It is a floating island.

ISLANDS

1

b.
Greenland covers 2,166,086 km², but only has a population of 56,452. Australia is larger but it is considered a continent rather than a true island.

2

c.
Great Britain is one of the British Isles, a group of islands which also includes Ireland, Shetland, the Isle of Man and many others.

3

a.
Due to rising sea levels, the Maldives could one day disappear underwater.

4

b.
The moai statues on Easter Island were carved from around 1250–1680 AD and weigh up to 82 tonnes.

5

True.
The state of Hawaii is home to over 130 islands.

DID YOU KNOW?

The word 'archipelago' literally means 'chief sea' in Greek, but archipelagos don't have to be formed in the sea – sometimes they occur in lakes and rivers too.

6

a.
An archipelago is a collection of islands.

7

a.
The Flevopolder is a huge area of reclaimed land covering 970 km², which is bigger than the Isle of Man and the Isle of Wight put together!

8

a.
The Norwegian archipelago has over 267,000 islands and reefs.

9

False.
East Island in Hawaii was completely washed away by a hurricane.

10

b.
Vulcan Point sits in Crater Lake, which lies on Volcano Island. Volcano Island sits in Lake Taal, and Lake Taal is located within the island of Luzon!

1 The City Montessori School in Lucknow, India is the biggest school in the world. Around how many pupils does it have?

a. 50

b. 5000

c. 55,000

2 London Waterloo railway station has the most platforms in the world.

True or false?

3 What is the world's most visited amusement park?

a. The Magic Kingdom, US

b. Alton Towers, UK

c. Disneyland Paris, France

4 The First World Hotel in Malaysia is the largest hotel in the world. How many bedrooms does it have?

a. 135

b. 7351

c. 27,351

5 The tallest statue in the world, the Statue of Unity in India, is taller than Blackpool Tower.

True or false?

6 What is the largest city in the world?

a. London, UK

b. Tokyo, Japan

c. New York, USA

7 Big Ben in London is the world's tallest clock.

True or false?

8 The largest swimming pool in the world is at the San Alfonso del Mar private resort in Chile. It is as big as...

a. 3 football pitches

b. 7 football pitches

c. 11 football pitches

9 How many diners can sit down to dinner together at the world's largest restaurant?

a. 6014

b. 604

c. 114

10 Stretching for 2.16 km, this is the longest pleasure pier in the world. Where is it?

a. Dubai, UAE

b. Florida, USA

c. Southend-on-Sea, England

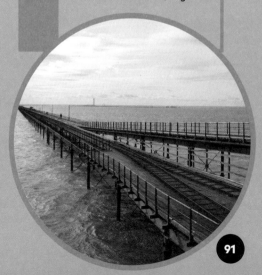

1

c.
There are more than 1000 classrooms in The City Montessori School in Lucknow, with a capacity to hold over 55,000 pupils.

HOTEL FIRST WORLD

2

False.
Grand Central Terminal in New York has 44 platforms, and it covers an area of 19 hectares.

4

b.
More than 35.5 million guests have stayed at the First World Hotel in Malaysia since it opened in 2006.

3

a.
The Magic Kingdom in Florida is visited by almost 21 million people a year.

5

True.
At 182 metres high, the statue is 24 metres taller than Blackpool Tower.

DID YOU KNOW?
More than 1 million fireworks are set off every year to illuminate the sky above the Magic Kingdom.

6

b.
The capital of Japan is the world's biggest city by area and population.

7

False.
The Makkah clock tower in Mecca is the tallest, measuring 601 m. The clock faces are the largest in the world, measuring 43 m across.

8

c.
The pool is 1013 m long and holds 250 million litres of water.

9

a.
The Damascus Gate Restaurant in Damascus can seat 6014 diners and also has 1800 staff.

10

c.
Southend pier in England is so long that it has its own railway line.

FROZEN POLES

TRUE or FALSE

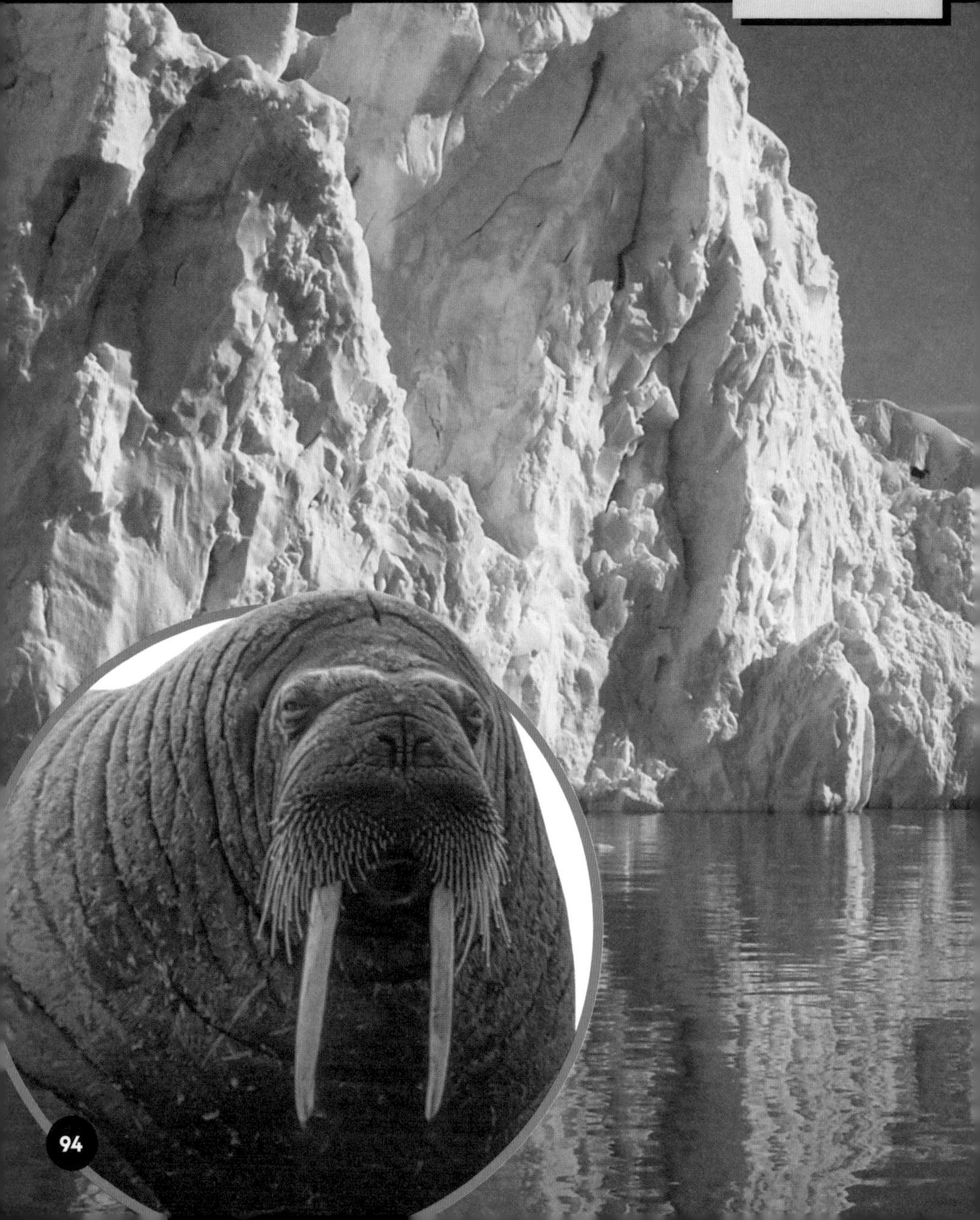

1 The lowest temperature ever recorded on Earth was at the North Pole.

2 Polar bears are the largest species of bear.

3 The northernmost marathon on Earth is run at the North Pole.

4 The first person to reach the South Pole was Captain Robert Scott in 1912.

5 There are no penguins in the Arctic.

6 The Arctic tern migrates from the Arctic all the way to the Antarctic and back again every year.

7 The Arctic-dwelling animal opposite is an elephant seal.

8 The largest-ever iceberg was bigger than the island of Jamaica.

9 The Southern Ocean is the only ocean that goes all the way round the globe.

10 In 1958, a submarine made the first ever undersea visit to the North Pole.

FROZEN POLES

1

FALSE.
The record low of
−89.2°C was set
in Antarctica in
1983.

2

TRUE.
Adult male
polar bears can
weigh 700 kg.

3

TRUE.
The North Pole
Marathon was first
run as a race in
2003.

4

FALSE.
Scott did reach the
South Pole in 1912
but a team led by
Roald Amundsen
had got there
5 weeks earlier.

5

TRUE.
Penguins are
only found in
the southern
hemisphere.

6

TRUE.
Arctic terns make
the longest
migrations in the
animal kingdom
with some terns
travelling
90,000 km a year.

7

FALSE.
It is a walrus.

8

TRUE.
Iceberg B-15 was
295 km long and
37 km wide, with
a surface area of
11,000 km².

9

TRUE.
The Southern
Ocean is a very
cold and windy
ocean, but it is rich
in sea life.

10

TRUE.
USS *Nautilus* was the first nuclear-powered submarine and it
could stay submerged much longer than previous submarines.

CONNECT FOUR

Four different examples, but what is the connection?

1 gold • diamond • coal • open-cast

2 Hinduism • Christianity • Islam • Buddhism

3 cumulus • cirrus • stratus • nimbus

4 Sahara • Atacama • Kalahari • Gobi

5 yen • sterling • rupee • dollar

6 humpback • minke • beluga • blue

7 Danube • Amazon • Nile • Mississippi

8 Table • Matterhorn • K2 • Kilimanjaro

9 Caspian • Aral • Mediterranean • North

10 Europe • Africa • Asia • Antarctica

CONNECT FOUR

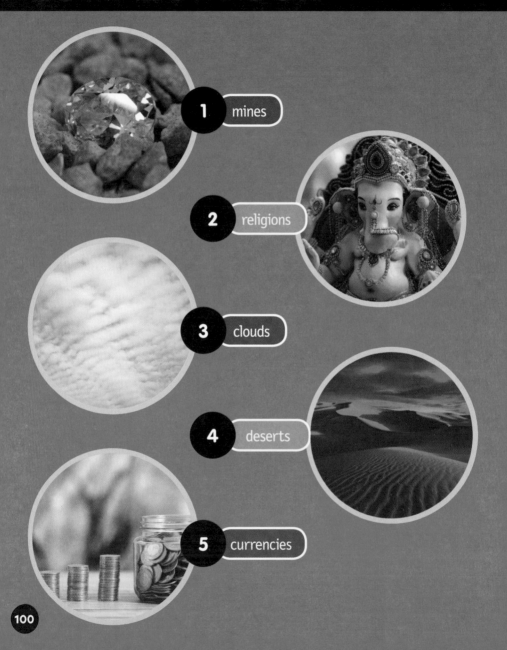

1 mines

2 religions

3 clouds

4 deserts

5 currencies

6 whales

7 rivers

8 mountains

9 seas

10 continents

COMPUTERS AND TECHNOLOGY

1 The Antikythera mechanism was thought to be the first type of computer. But who used it?

a. The Tudors
b. The Ancient Greeks
c. The Victorians

2 Which of these is NOT a computer programming language?

a. Python   b. Java   c. Pirate

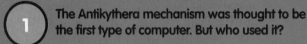

3 The average smartphone has over a million times more memory than the computer in the Apollo 11 spacecraft that made the first manned landing on the Moon.

True or false?

4 How many calculations can the world's fastest supercomputer make in a second?

a. 415 billion   b. 415 trillion   c. 415 quadrillion

5 What was the first computer mouse made of?

a. Wood   b. Cheese   c. Fur

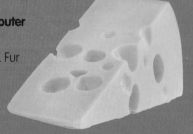

6 The video game industry now makes more money than the movie industry.
True or false?

 7 What is this very popular piece of technology (right) called?
a. Mobile phone
b. Drone
c. Helicopter

 8 What is the best-selling games console of all time?
a. Nintendo Switch   b. PlayStation 2   c. Xbox 360

 9 What test would a computer have to pass to show it has artificial intelligence?
a. Turing test   b. Litmus test   c. Driving test

 10 Robots have been invented that can play which of these games?
a. Table tennis   b. Jenga   c. Football

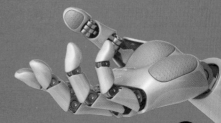

COMPUTERS AND TECHNOLOGY

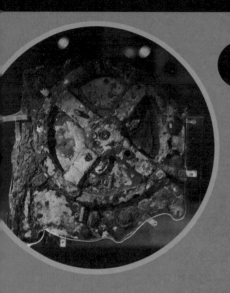

1

b.
The Antikythera mechanism is thought to have helped the Ancient Greeks calculate and show information about all things astronomical, like the Sun, Moon, planets and stars.

2

c.
There are around 700 programming languages, but Pirate isn't one of them.

3

True.
The Apollo 11 computer had 4 kilobytes of RAM – an average mobile phone has 4 gigabytes of RAM, which is a million times more.

4

c.
The Fugaku supercomputer in Japan has clocked 415 petaflops – equivalent to 415 quadrillion (a million billion) calculations per second.

5

a.
The mouse was invented by Douglas Engelbart in 1964. It got its name because the wire made it look like a mouse with a tail.

6 **True.**
In 2019, the gaming industry was worth around $150 billion. The global box office that year was around $42 billion.

7 **b.**
There are thousands of uses for drones – some people even race them.

8 **b.**
The PlayStation 2 was launched in 2000 and has sold more than the Xbox 360 and the Switch combined.

9 **a.**
The Turing test is named after computer scientist Alan Turing. To pass the test, a computer has to answer questions like a human would.

10 **a, b and c.**
There is also a robot that can do kung fu!

TRANSPORT

1

The world's first underground railway opened in 1863 underneath which city?

a. New York

b. London

c. Edinburgh

2

The motor car was invented in 1885 by whom?

a. Karl Benz

b. Henry Ford

c. Fred Mercedes

3

When cars were first invented, they needed someone to walk in front and wave a red flag to warn everyone that they were coming.

True or false?

4

What was the name of the largest-ever airship?

a. *Boaty McBoatface*

b. *Lightning McQueen*

c. *Hindenburg*

5

What does this road sign indicate?

a. Turn around

b. Roundabout

c. Beware of vehicles driving in circles

6

How is the form of transport know as a palanquin powered?

a. Coal

b. Oil

c. Humans

7

What is Japan's superfast train known as in English?

a. Bullet train

b. Thomas the Tank Engine

c. The noodle

8

What is a tuk tuk?

a. A motorised rickshaw

b. A kind of scooter

c. A small boat

9

How many cats and dogs have travelled through the Channel Tunnel since it opened?

a. None—cats and dogs aren't allowed in it

b. 500

c. Over 2 million

10

Which country has the most cyclists relative to its size?

a. China

b. Denmark

c. The Netherlands

1

b. It opened as the 'Metropolitan Railway' but is now known as the London Underground, or 'the Tube'.

2

a. The first version of Karl Benz's car was difficult to control, and crashed into a wall during a public demonstration.

3

True. The law that made this rule was called the Red Flag Act.

4

c. The *Hindenburg* sadly caught fire and crashed in 1937. It used flammable hydrogen for lift instead of helium.

5

b. The sign shows that there is a roundabout ahead, and the direction in which you should travel around it.

6

c. A palanquin is a type of litter, a box for one passenger carried by people using poles.

7

a. The Japanese name for the Bullet train is Shinkansen. These trains travel nearly twice as fast as the fastest trains in the UK!

8

a. These three-wheeled vehicles are used in busy cities like Bangkok, and get their name from the sound they make.

9

c. Cats and dogs need their own passports to travel abroad, and so do ferrets!

10

c. The Netherlands has 16.6 million citizens and 99.1% of them own a bike.

SPORT

1

What sport takes place at Silverstone?
a. Boxing
b. Rugby
c. Motor racing

2

Which athlete has won the most Olympic medals ever?
a. Sprinter Usain Bolt
b. Swimmer Michael Phelps
c. Cyclist Chris Hoy

3

What colour is the centre of an archery target?
a. Black
b. Red
c. Gold

4

Which of these sports is NOT played using a racket?
a. Tennis
b. Hockey
c. Squash

5

What sport uses a shuttlecock?
a. Badminton
b. Quidditch
c. Chicken racing

6

In which sport do players slide rocks across an ice rink?

a. Marbles

b. Shot put

c. Curling

7

Rank these golf scores from best to least good.

a. Birdie

b. Albatross

c. Eagle

8

Footballs were originally made of pigs' bladders.

True or false?

9

What is this famous English sporting venue (left)?

a. Wimbledon

b. Lords

c. Wembley

10

How many points do you get for scoring a try in rugby union?

a. 4

b. 5

c. 6

DID YOU KNOW?

Golf balls have an average of 336 dimples.

SPORT

1

c. Silverstone is a famous racetrack in England.

2

b. Michael Phelps has won 28 Olympic medals – the next-best total is 18.

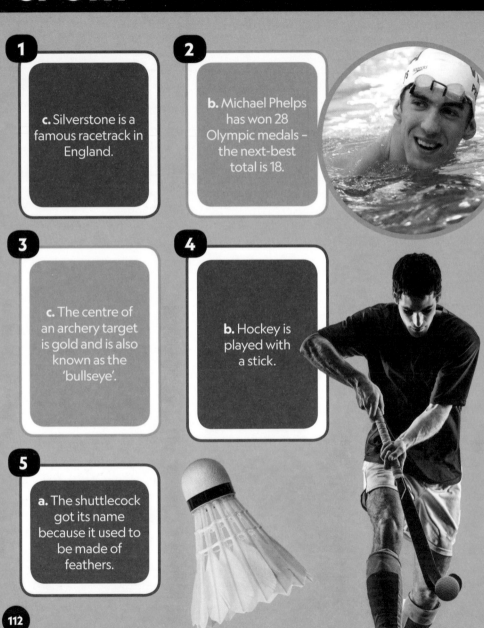

3

c. The centre of an archery target is gold and is also known as the 'bullseye'.

4

b. Hockey is played with a stick.

5

a. The shuttlecock got its name because it used to be made of feathers.

6

c. Rocks is another name for curling stones, which players slide across the ice curling sheet towards a circular target called the house.

7

BEST
a. Birdie
(1 under par)
c. Eagle
(2 under par)
b. Albatross
(3 under par)
LEAST GOOD

8

True.
Sometimes sheep's bladders were used too.

9

a. The Wimbledon tennis championship is the oldest in the world.

10

b. The score for a try was increased from 4 points to 5 in 1992.

ELEMENTS

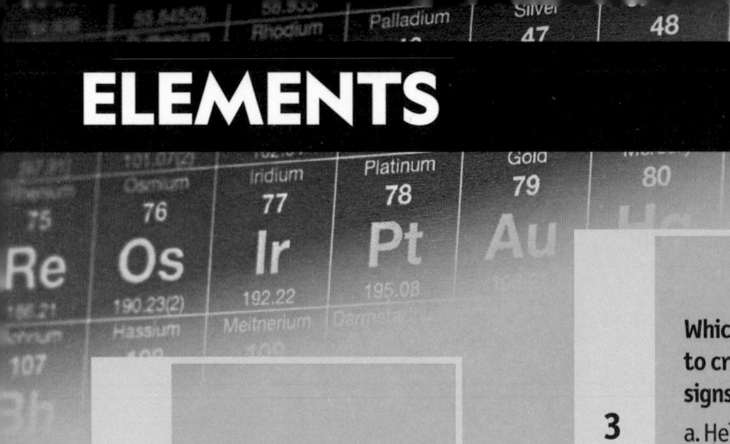

1 What is the symbol for oxygen?

a. O   b. On   c. Z

2 What is the lightest element?

a. Oxygen
b. Magnesium
c. Hydrogen

3 Which gas is put in tubes to create advertising signs that light up?

a. Helium
b. Oxygen
c. Neon

4 Silver is heavier than gold.

True or false?

5 The planet Mars contains the same elements as Earth.

True or false?

6 What is the liquid metal element called on the right?

a. Copper

b. Mercury

c. Lead

7 The village of Ytterby in Sweden has 4 elements named after it.

True or false?

8 Which of these is not a real element?

a. Einsteinium

b. Darwinium

c. Lawrencium

9 Helium is used to make wedding rings.

True or false?

10 The table salt that we put on our food is made up of a toxic metal element and a poisonous gas element.

True or false?

1 a. Oxygen's symbol is 'O'. Almost all living creatures —including humans— need oxygen in order to survive.

2 c. Hydrogen is the lightest element and also the most abundant chemical substance in the universe.

3 c. Neon glows when it is placed in an electric field.

4 False. Gold is nearly twice as heavy as silver.

5 True. Though the two planets have differing amounts of the individual elements.

DID YOU KNOW?

Without hydrogen, life cannot exist because hydrogen forms a part of nearly all the molecules that make up living things.

6 **b.** Mercury is the only metallic element that is liquid at room temperature.

8 **b.** Darwinium is made up, but a. and c. were named after famous scientists.

7 **True.** The elements yttrium, erbium, terbium and ytterbium are all named after Ytterby, where they were first discovered. Four more elements were also unearthed there!

9 **False.** Helium is a light gas. One of its uses is inflating balloons and making them float!

10 **True.** Salt crystals form when sodium (a toxic metal) and chlorine (a poisonous gas) combine to make sodium chloride—which is only poisonous in very high quantities!

BRIDGES AND TUNNELS

1

The tallest bridge in the world is in France.

2

A pontoon bridge is a bridge that floats.

3

There is a pedestrian bridge in China that has a glass walkway.

4

The Golden Gate Bridge in San Francisco is the world's longest suspension bridge.

5

One of the oldest bridges in the world is still in use in Somerset, England.

6

The largest bridge made out of Lego is nearly as long as three double-decker buses.

7

The photo on the left is of London Bridge.

8

The Forth Bridge is a famous railway bridge in Ireland.

9

The Channel Tunnel is the longest undersea tunnel in the world.

10

A bascule bridge is a type of bridge that can lift its spans up to let boats pass through.

BRIDGES AND TUNNELS

TRUE or FALSE

1

TRUE.
The Millau Viaduct in France is 336.4 metres tall.

2

TRUE.
Pontoon bridges use a roadway laid on top of floats.

3

TRUE.
To prove the glass bridge is safe, officials hit it with sledgehammers and drove a car filled with passengers over it.

4

FALSE.
The Golden Gate Bridge in San Francisco was the longest suspension bridge when it opened in 1937 but has been surpassed. The Akashi Kaikyō Bridge in Japan holds the current record with a span of 1991 m.

5

TRUE.
The Tarr Steps bridge in Exmoor National Park may have been built as early as 1400 BC.

6

TRUE.
It is made from 200,000 Lego bricks.

7

FALSE.
It is Tower Bridge, which is in London but is different from London Bridge which is a crossing further upriver.

8

FALSE.
The Forth Bridge is in Scotland.

9

TRUE.
The Channel Tunnel runs for 37.9 kilometres under the sea – no other tunnel has a longer underwater section.

10

TRUE.
A bascule bridge is also called a lifting bridge.

MEGA MACHINES

1 **What makes the Troll A gas platform particularly notable?**
a. It is home to thousands of trolls.
b. It produces more gas than any other platform in the world.
c. It is the tallest and heaviest structure that has ever been moved by humans.

2 **What is the nickname of the largest crane in the world?**
a. Wee Steve   b. Big Carl   c. Craney McCraneface

3 **Once the largest self-propelled land vehicle in the world, what did the Crawler-Transporter transport?**
a. Nothing   b. Space rockets   c. Elephants

4 **A bicycle is a machine.**
True or false?

5 **What does the mega machine on the left do?**
a. It cleans the sides of ships.
b. It bores tunnels.
c. It rolls out pastry for giant pies.

6 **What is the name of the world's largest tunnel-boring machine?**
a. Anna   b. Elsa   c. Bertha

7 **The world's largest wind turbine is as tall as the Eiffel Tower.** True or false?

8 **What is 'La Princesse'?**
a. A robot princess
b. A giant mechanical spider
c. A combine harvester

9 **The most expensive machine ever built is the International Space Station.**
True or false?

10 **The largest machine in the world is 27 km in circumference. What was it built to do?**
a. It makes cars.
b. It studies subatomic particles.
c. It stops volcanoes erupting.

MEGA MACHINES

1 **c.** Troll A is 472 metres tall and weighs 683,600 tonnes.

2 **b.** Big Carl can carry 5000 tonnes in a single lift. That's the weight of about 400 double-decker buses!

3 **b.** These NASA vehicles moved Saturn V rockets and space shuttles from their assembly building to their launch site.

4 **True.** Machines help make things easier for us. Bicycles help us travel from A to B more quickly than walking.

5 **b.** The Crossrail project in London used eight of these tunnel-boring machines to gouge out its tunnels.

6   **c.** Bertha was built in Japan and has a diameter of 17.5 metres.

7   **False.** It's not quite as tall as the Eiffel Tower. The turbine's hub is 150 m above the ground and its blade tips reach 220 m.

8   **b.** The 15-metre mechanical spider needed a crew of twelve people to operate her in a street theatre performance.

9   **True.** The final cost of the space station will be over $150 billion (£77.8 billion). It is the most expensive object ever made.

10   **b.** The largest machine ever built by humans is the Large Hadron Collider, which was built to study some of the smallest things in existence. The particle collider is buried 100 m under the ground near Geneva, Switzerland.

TIE BREAKER

If there's a draw between two players, try this tie breaker question...
closest answer wins!

MONT BLANC IS THE HIGHEST PEAK IN THE ALPS. HOW TALL IS IT, IN METRES?

Mont Blanc is 4810 metres tall.

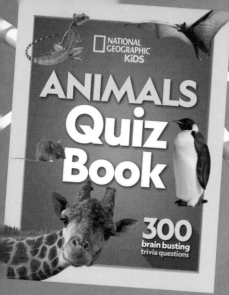

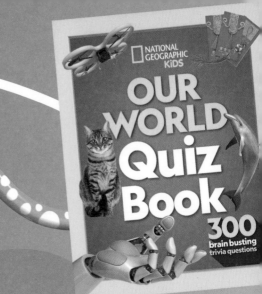

NATIONAL GEOGRAPHIC KiDS

Quiz books

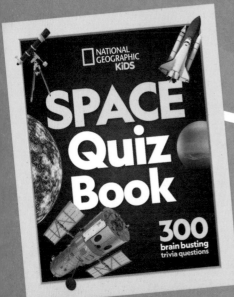

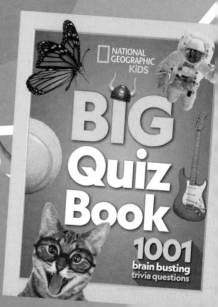